Am

A P
for visitors

Compiled by "Cumbria"
Illustrated by J. J. Thomlinson

The Old Mill

DALESMAN BOOKS
1977

35p.

THE DALESMAN PUBLISHING COMPANY LTD.,
CLAPHAM (via Lancaster), NORTH YORKSHIRE

First Published 1977

ISBN : O 85206 392 X

Printed in Great Britain by
GEO. TODD & SON,
Marlborough Street, Whitehaven.

CONTENTS

Fox How, Ambleside

INTRODUCING AMBLESIDE

WELL over half the day-trippers who visit Lakeland spend an appreciable amount of time at Ambleside and Windermere, close to England's largest lake. Tourism came to Ambleside as its old market declined; prior to that it was an insignificant hamlet.

Consider the location of this thriving town. Ambleside faces south, into the summer sun. Look in that direction and you discover that the big lake, Windermere, is near at hand and that the hills around it are of modest elevation, for this is Silurian country. Yet, on the other three sides of Ambleside, rise hills that command attention; to the north, Nab Scar (1,300 feet), Fairfield (2,863 feet) and High Pike (2,000 feet); to the east, Red Screes (2,541 feet) and Wansfell (1,597 feet); to the west, Loughrigg (1,101 feet). John Wesley, coming this way for the first time in 1751, passed through Ambleside and then "over more than

The Market Place

Welsh mountains". Today the highway is the main trunk road of Lakeland.

Moving ice created the low country around Ambleside by gouging the landscape. Ice of the last great period of glaciation reached the area from the Langdales and Helvellyn and, combining with ice from the Troutbeck valley, deepened the main valley to such an extent that a considerable depth of water was retained: hence Windermere. The folk who first colonised the Ambleside area would use the lake as a watery way to the south; they would also lift from it a variety of fish. The species that has the greatest interest for visitors is known as the char, which was presumably migratory — as is the salmon — but became landlocked in the Ice Age of some 14,000 years ago.

When the Romans found it necessary to police the Lake District, then the home of a few native tribes, they constructed a fort at Borrans, near the present-day Waterhead, and here was also to be found a large civil settlement. The name Ambleside is said to be associated with a Norseman called Hamel, a notion challenged by another authority who interprets it as "a shieling on a sandbank by a river". The name in its present spelling was being generally used in the 15th century.

An old record describes Ambleside as lying "in the forest of Troutbeck — near to the forest of Rydal, where the twin valleys of Rothay and Brathay meet". The main local river is the Rothay, which takes water from the Scandale and Stock becks. Wild greylag geese, flying south in autumn over the main Lakeland passes, are periodically seen by watchers at Ambleside. Even the golden eagle has been observed as it soared high above the town. The creature most commonly seen in this district is the sheep; the sheep stock of years ago provided wool for local industries and sustained a market at Ambleside. Water tumbling from high hills gave the power for the early fulling mills.

As the market declined, Ambleside was saved by tourism. At first it was select, patronised by the new rich of the towns and, later, by literary personalities. William Green, who wrote a guide to Lakeland in two volumes that was one of the earliest of its type, used Ambleside as his base. Hartley Coleridge lived here. Harriet Martineau built The

Smithy Brow, Ambleside

Knoll, and Dr. Arnold, the famous headmaster of Rugby, found a pleasant home at Fox How.

The older houses of Ambleside — and the church of St. Anne, now a parochial hall — cling to the higher land, and when built, were kept well clear of the marshy vale. When Ambleside began to spread with the tourist boom of the mid-19th century, a number of wealthy families decided to build houses here. Hotels and terraces of large houses also appeared on the lower ground that was hitherto shunned. The busiest period of building work came a few years after Windermere's fantastic growth on the arrival of the railway in 1847.

Today, Ambleside presents a largely Victorian appearance to the visitor, yet he need not look far to see evidence of the former town. It speaks well for local government that Ambleside's council estates are inconspicuous. Being near the heart of a National Park, every development is closely scrutinised and a special planning board has strict rules about the type of material used.

Students of architecture will spend most of their time considering such structures as the Bridge House, the old mill or the majestic Victorian church of St. Mary, but consideration might also be given to a building development at Kirkfield, not far from the old chapel of St. Anne, in the high-lying part of town. Until recent times, the land was used for grazing stock; it was the lower fell type, with large boulders strewn about it, and a beck flowing through. The development, initially of 44 dwellings, won a medal for good design in housing in 1975.

Paths lead from Ambleside to the high fells. Minor roads can be followed to interesting places. And down at Waterhead, the graceful white boats of *Sealink* arrive at the pier, maintaining a service that began long ago. Early this century, it was possible for a visitor to Blackpool to enjoy a remarkable day trip that included tea at Ambleside. That visitor was conveyed across Morecambe Bay from Fleetwood to Barrow by steamer, and a railway train took him or her on to Lakeside, where a steamer was boarded for a sail to Waterhead. After enjoying a brief interlude at Ambleside, the visitor was taken by coach to Coniston, where a train was used for the return to Barrow. Here the steamer was moored, ready for the return crossing of Morecambe Bay to Fleetwood.

Waterhead, a popular boating centre

GENERAL INFORMATION

AMBLESIDE is in the county of Cumbria. The town lies five miles from Windermere station and 17 miles from Keswick. Ullswater is a mere 10 miles away, across the Kirkstone Pass. Grasmere, strongly associated with Wordsworth, is within comfortable walking distance at four miles. Dungeon Ghyll, near the head of Great Langdale, lies eight miles from Ambleside.

Early closing day: Thursday, though most shops remain open on this day during the June to October holiday season.

Rainfall: Yearly average 73 inches. On average, the sun shines at Ambleside for 1,170 hours.

Car Parks: Kelsick Road, Lake Road, Low Fold, Rydal Road, Waterhead. A park at Waterhead was created by the Lake District Planning Board.

Information: At the Bridge House (National Trust) and the Lake District National Park Information Service, Church Street (Ambleside 3084). An accommodation bureau is organised by the local Publicity Association.

Police Station: Rydal Road.

Council Offices: Rothay Holme.

Post Office: Market Place.

Public Library: Kelsick Road.

Bus Tours: Brown's Coaches, Market Place (Tel. : 2205). Whole day coach tours include Wastwater and Buttermere, Eight Lakes, Ullswater and Appleby. Minibus Tours to Buttermere, via Borrowdale and Honister, also Ullswater and Haweswater, and other areas. Consult the firm's brochure. Another enterprise, by the Windermere-based "Mountain Goat", offers a number of regular service runs by minibus, including one that crosses Kirkstone Pass from Ambleside and Windermere to reach Glenridding by Ullswater, and a run across the Wrynose and Hardknott passes to Eskdale and Wasdale.

Main Bus Station: Ribble Motor Services, Ltd.

Railway: Nearest station is at Windermere, but *Sealink* (British Railways) operates a big-boat service in the holiday season throughout the length of Windermere lake, calling at the pier at Waterhead.

Cricket: Games played at Rydal each Saturday and on occasional Sundays.

Tennis: Hard and grass courts at White Platts; daily except Sunday.

Bowls: Council-owned green at White Platts. Ambleside Bowling Club's green is at Rothay Holme.

Hunting: A winter pursuit. The Coniston Foxhounds visit the Ambleside area.

Angling: Consult a local tackle dealer or the boatmen at Waterhead. A river authority licence can be obtained from the Ambleside Motor Launch Company at Waterhead. No licence is needed for coarse fishing in the lakes. A tackle dealer will inform a visitor about the angling facilities offered by the local angling association.

Boating: Waterhead Bay.

Caravan sites: White Cross Bay (south of town) and Skelwith Fold (by the road from Ambleside to Hawkshead); also a number of local farms by arrangement.

Sports Events: Ambleside Sports at Rydal Park (Thursday preceding the first Monday in August); Grasmere Sports (third or fourth Thursday in August); Vale of Rydal Sheep Dog Trials (second Thursday in August).

Rushbearing: Linked with St. Anne's Day, July 26, but now held on the Saturday nearest to July 2. Grasmere's Rushbearing is held on the Saturday nearest to St. Oswald's Day, which is usually the first Saturday of August.

Churches: St. Mary's Parish Church; Methodist Church; Roman Catholic Church; Christian Brethren.

The Queen's Pavilion

AMBLESIDE IN HISTORY

A Chronological Summary

79 The Romans arrive, building a fort of wood and clay at what is now Borrans. (A more substantial fort is constructed about 20 years later; the Romans abandon their position c400 A.D.)

1189 Granting by Richard II to Gilbert Fitz Reinfrid of the forest of "Westmarieland", Kendal and Furness; it includes Windermere.

1275 The settlement "Above Stock", or what is now old Ambleside, is now in the parish of Grasmere, being referred to as Amelsate.

1324 The hamlet, now written of as Hamelsate, is stated to have a corn mill.

1494 Thomas Braithwaite owns a fulling mill at Ambleside.

c1550 A small chapel is being used at Ambleside.

1636 The valuation of village rents produces a total of £24.

1650 Ambleside becomes a market town. The first charter allows for a weekly market (wool and general produce) and two fairs. (Another charter, awarded by James II in 1688, includes power to collect tolls for the benefit of the poor.)

1676 The village becomes an ecclesiastical parish; it is no longer dependent on Grasmere.

1718 A large part of Ambleside and its district is sold by Lady Otway to a Mr. Dummer for £1,750.

c1723 A Free Grammar School is opened.

1760s Coming of a turnpike road. (In due course, a six-horse coach rumbles through Ambleside, on its way from Kendal to Carlisle. The journey takes six hours.)

1791 There are five ale-houses at Ambleside. Four are known: **The Unicorn, Salutation, White Lion** and **Fox and Goose.**

1812 St. Anne's church is opened; it occupies the site of the 16th century chapel.

1813 William Wordsworth, of Rydal, becomes the Distributor of Stamps for Westmorland, having his office at Ambleside.

1823 Hartley Coleridge moves into town (and remains here until about 1830).

c1825 The weekly market lapses (to be revived in the 1970s).

1833 Dr. Arnold, of Rugby School, is at Fox How.

1835 The Rev. Owen Lloyd writes the hymn that is henceforth used at Ambleside Rushbearing. Harriet Martineau takes up residence at The Knoll (until her death in 1876).

1845 Windermere Steam Yacht Company is founded (until this date, the only regular communication up and down the lake has been by passage boats).

1847 Opening of the rail link from the south to Windermere. The number of tourists in Ambleside begins to increase dramatically.

1854 Opening of St. Mary's church, Ambleside.

1863 The Market Hall replaces The Cross House.

1894 Charlotte Mason opens a House of Education; she has bought the property known as Scale How.

1926 The Bridge House is purchased by public subscription. (It is handed over to the National Trust, who use it as an information and recruitment centre.)

1944 Gordon Ransome paints the Rushbearing mural at St. Mary's church.

WALKING THROUGH AMBLESIDE

WE start on the hill, in that part of Ambleside known as "Above Stock". Looking at the huddled old buildings you will have a good idea of what the old town was like. From here we meander down to Waterhead.

Kirkstone Pass: If you feel energetic, leave the top end of Ambleside for a walk to Kirkstone Pass. The distance from the market cross to the Pass is about three miles. During that distance you will gain in elevation about 1,300 feet. The road is known as The Struggle, and struggle was the key word in the days when horse-drawn coaches operated a summer excursion programme up and across to Patterdale. Kirkstone lies at 1,476 feet, with a famous inn — *The Kirkstone Pass* — not quite at the summit. (Visitors going by car may return to Ambleside by the main road, which passes through the long and attractive Troutbeck valley to Windermere town.)

Kirkfield: Consider for a while the new estate beside the road to Kirkstone; it lies not far from the old church of St. Anne. Kirkfield was intended to be low-cost public housing, but it has a different appearance from the norm, being architect-designed, echoing the Cumbrian style of building. The beck running through the site was well exploited, and good use made of local stone in the landscaping.

St. Anne's: Also known as The Old Church. Now used as a church hall, St. Anne's served the parish for many years until the construction of St. Mary's on low ground. St. Anne's dates back to 1812, succeeding a chapel of 16th century date. Rushes strewn on the floor were annually renewed; hence the Rushbearing held at Ambleside to this day. In the yard of St. Anne's is the tombstone of the Rev. John Dawes, parson from 1811-45.

How Head: This venerable building is a close neighbour of St. Anne's. Historians date How Head to the 16th century and associate it with the Braithwaite family. It is related that some stone from the Roman fort at Borrans was used in its construction. A considerable amount of stone was needed. How Head impresses with its massive form and substantial circular chimneys.

St. Anne's — the old church

The Old Mill: Just off North Road. Formerly a corn mill, it was owned for many years by the Braithwaite family. The present waterwheel (which dates from 1973) is a faithful reproduction of the old, being 16 feet in diameter and 40 inches wide, supported on an oaken shaft 18 inches thick. The Old Mill is now a pottery. Visitors are welcome.

The Market Place: The first market charter dates back to 1650, a second being awarded in 1688. The market lapsed, to be reintroduced in recent years. The cross, a sandstone obelisk, formerly stood near the market hall.

Bridge House: The present road to Rydal was made in 1843. Prior to this the Old Bridge House, Ambleside's best known building, was well clear of traffic. The bridge connected the gardens of the former Ambleside Hall to an orchard lying across the beck. It is believed to be of 17th century date. After its days as a summer house, it became a counting house connected with the former cloth mill of the Stock Gill. In the 1850s, Bridge House was the home of a family called Rigg. A local story asserts that the last head of this family reared six children in the meagre accommodation. For a time, early this century, a cobbler used the premises; the top room was simply a pigeon loft. Then the Bridge House became an antique and gift shop. In 1926, local people subscribed £450 to purchase the building, which was then handed over to the National Trust. In 1956, it was opened as the Trust's first information and recruitment centre in England. Today, the curious building has an isolated appearance, with the busy main road only a few feet away, but a drawing of 1821 shows it surrounded by rockery, grass and trees. Incidentally, the principal room of the Bridge House is only about 13 feet by 6 feet in size.

The Knoll: Just off the Rydal road. The Knoll, which is private property, is interesting because it was planned by Harriet Martineau and she lived here from 1846 until her death in 1876. She was the friend of many notable people, and among the visitors to The Knoll was Charlotte Brontë. As a writer on political and social topics, she became extremely well known throughout the land.

"The Salutation," which dates back to the 17th century

Charlotte Mason College: Clearly seen from the Rydal road, the building is a notable college of education that began towards the end of last century as a House of Education. Charlotte Mason (1842-1923) had come to know and love Ambleside in 1864; she admired its beauty and literary associations and once called it "an unwalled university". Here was a quiet place where the students might prepare for their high vocation by learning of the nature and the needs of children at first hand. She said to one of her students: "You have come here to learn — not to teach, but how to live".

Salutation Hotel: This prominent hostelry dates back to the mid-17th century. In the early tourist age, it became an important centre for visitors, providing horses and vehicles for excursions into the district around the town.

The Library: Kelsick Road. To it was transferred the Armitt Library, founded by Mary Louisa Armitt and opened in 1912. Miss Armitt wanted to provide a "collection of books of scientific, literary, or antiquarian value, which may be made available to the student and to the book-lover". Local books figure prominently in the collection.

St. Mary's Church: Anyone who sees this church must have the impression that its designer, Gilbert Scott, attempted to compete with nature herself — to create, indeed, something as imposing as the fells that form a semi-circle round the town. The spire of St. Mary's extends to 180 feet. The church construction took four years; it was consecrated in June 1854 and has all the stolid self-assurance of the Victorian age during which the town developed furiously. It is said that Wordsworth selected the site for the church; he was certainly interested in the plans but he died before construction work began. The church stands on solid rock — so solid, indeed, that when a new vestry was being made in 1968 workmen tackled a great lump of rock with pneumatic drills. Inside the church are reminders — usually in the form of stained glass windows — of the great Victorian families of the district. The Wordsworth Chapel is an attraction for many. Friends and admirers of the poet's work living in this country and America subscribed towards the cost of a window, and in 1952, during celebrations to mark the centenary of the poet's death, this part of the church was furnished as a chapel. In it are two chairs that adorned the poet's home at Rydal Mount. Windows in the south aisle of St. Mary's commemorate the Lutwidge family, especially Captain Lutwidge. His wife laid the foundation stone of the church. What is known as the children's window (to the west of the south door) was placed there by public subscription in 1889 to commemorate W. E. Forster and Matthew Arnold, two men who contributed to educational reform. The Arnolds lived at Fox How.

The Rushbearing: It is appropriate here to mention an old Ambleside custom, the Rushbearing. Within moments of entering St. Mary's, the eye focusses on a painting 26 feet long and about 12 feet high. It uses the Rushbearing as its theme and has 62 almost life-sized figures, including portraits of the vicar and verger who were in office when the mural was painted by Gordon Ransome, a student at the Royal College of Art — the College had its headquarters in Ambleside during the 1939-45 war. Years ago, the earthen floors of many country churches were strewn with fresh rushes in summer; it was a time of joyous celebration. The custom of Rushbearing at the old church, St. Anne's, endured when that church was rebuilt and flagged in 1812. In 1835, the Rushbearing was stylised by the curate, Owen Lloyd. This fascinating person was originally a Quaker, son of Charles Lloyd of Brathay. He was baptised as an adult, confirmed and then ordained in the Church of England. Lloyd composed a Rushbearing hymn which is still used. Today, reeds and rushes gathered from the lakes and tarns are woven with flowers on to wooden frames of various designs, being referred to as "bearings". A procession begins at the school near St. Mary's and tours the town to the market place; it is here that the special hymn is sung. Then all the bearings are lifted high for a moment for the assembled crowd to see. The procession continues, and a service is held in church. When the service is over, the bearings are left in church and all who have carried them receive gingerbread. On the day following, Sunday, further special services are held. The festival concludes on the Monday with a tea and sports for the children.

Rothay Park: Near St. Mary's church. Bounded by the Rothay, and preserving an appearance of naturalness, the park is for the use of the public; seats are provided. Rothay Bridge, lower down, is on the old road from Ambleside to Hawkshead. The route was featured in Clarke's *Survey of the Lakes* (1787).

Broadlands: The regional office of The National Trust. John Dawes once lived here; he had a school that was attended by Hartley Coleridge.

Borrans Park: Owned by the council, this attractive open space extends along the shore of Windermere, at the head of Waterhead Bay—seats are available for the visiting public.

The remains of Roman Ambleside lie in Borrans Field (20 acres) which was bought for The National Trust by public subscription in 1912. Two forts, one of Agricola's time, another in the time of Trajan, have been identified; the Roman name was Galava. The fort was linked with Hardknott to the west, with Kendal to the south and — via the route lying over the imposing fell named High Street — with Brough in the east. An explanatory leaflet is available. The site became derelict about 400 A.D.

How Head, in the oldest part of town

"The Tern," one of the "Sealink" vessels

THE LAKE

WINDERMERE is England's largest lake, being 10½ miles in length, though not very broad in proportion. The hills around it tend to be of only moderate height and rounded; they abound in native species of timber. In summer, the lake is warm on top and cold lower down, and the layers do not mix until autumn, when the surface water cools down. Windermere has a maximum depth of 219 feet.

The species of fish about which most has been written is the char which, in the case of Windermere, became land-locked at the time of the Ice Age. In normal conditions, char behave very much as do their relatives the salmon, spawning in fresh water and moving to the sea to feed and grow before undertaking a spawning run. Other fish in Windermere are brown trout, perch, eels and pike. One specimen of pike recovered from the lake weighed 33½ lb.

Incidentally, the bed of Windermere was presented to the local authority by Mr. H. Leigh Groves.

During the tourist season, Waterhead bustles with life. Here visitors can book for outings on the lake, or they can hire craft to explore the bay. To Ambleside Pier come the graceful white-hulled craft of *Sealink,* the marine section of British Rail. Over 700,000 people a year are conveyed on this freshwater fleet during the tourist season. The *Swift,* launched in 1900, is the longest of the craft, at 158 feet. Like her counterparts, she was once steam-driven but was converted to diesel. *Swan, Teal* and *Tern* are other vessels. *Swan* and *Teal,* which date from the 1930s, are each 140 feet 9 inches long. The *Tern,* which is 146 feet in length, is the most distinctive of the vessels, having canoe-shaped bows and being embossed with the legend of the bird.

Ambleside Pier

ROUND ABOUT AMBLESIDE

WALKING

Details of walks in the area are to be found in *Walking in Central Lakeland*, by Brian and Joy Greenwood (a *Dalesman Mini-Book* obtainable locally). Many rights of way are clearly signposted, and the National Park Centre at Brockhole, just south of Ambleside, has much helpful information. Above all, buy an Ordnance Survey map of reasonable scale on which the footpaths are clearly marked. Three recommended walks are to Loughrigg summit (beginning with a walk through Rothay Park and on via Pine Rigg and Tarn Foot), to Stock Ghyll (route begins behind the *Salutation Hotel* at Ambleside) and Scandale and Sweden Bridge (using Sweden Bridge Lane in Upper Ambleside).

THREE NATURE WALKS

Skelghyll Wood: An hour's walk arranged by the Ambleside Field Society and The National Trust, beginning opposite Waterhead Hotel (A591). An explanatory booklet is available locally. Adding half an hour to the time taken, a visitor can attain the outstanding vantage point of Jenkins Crag.

Rothay Valley and Loughrigg: A longer walk, some 2½ hours, arranged by the Charlotte Mason College of Education and the National Trust. Booklet available locally. Going can be rough, so stout footwear is necessary. The walk begins at the Old Bridge House in Rydal Road, Ambleside.

White Moss Common: Take a bus from Ambleside to White Moss Quarry, between Rydal and Grasmere. The Nature Walk has been arranged by the Cumbria Naturalists' Trust and The National Trust. A booklet is available. The walk will take about 45 minutes and it passes through wood, open fell and then more woodland. The more energetic can make a 45 minute detour along the shore of Grasmere.

TWO AMBLESIDE BRIDGES

Rothay Bridge

High Sweden Bridge

SHORT MOTOR RUNS

The Langdales: Take the road to Clappersgate, crossing the Rothay Bridge. *Brathay Hall,* to the left, is an adventure centre dedicated to providing courses for young people engaged in industry and commerce. The Georgian house is set in 350 acres of parkland and woodland extending to the shores of Windermere. As a matter of interest, the house dates from the 18th century. George Law, who put its construction in hand, used a site overlooking the lake which had been occupied by a small farmhouse. He faced his new home with pale yellow sandstone of a type not found in the locality, an act that moved S. T. Coleridge to describe the building as "a white palace". In 1939, the hall and estate were purchased from the Redmayne family by Francis Scott, of Matson Ground, Windermere, whose idea was to preserve it. The hall began its long period of experimentation and effort in the fields of education and industrial training in 1947.

At *White Craggs,* Clappersgate, is an outstanding rock garden made by the Hough family; it extends up the slopes of Loughrigg in what was formerly an area of coppice wood. The garden is open to the public, and visitors follow zig-zag paths through a richly floriferous area. Some plants sent by Reginald Farrer during expeditions to the Far East were given space at White Craggs. The garden is probably at its peak of beauty in spring, when masses of rhododendrons and azaleas are flowering. The local vantage points offer long views of Windermere and its wooded hills.

Elterwater: Here the roads run on unenclosed land where you will see Herdwicks, the native sheep of the Lake District. The village was formerly a busy centre for charcoal-burning and gunpowder production. It also has some impressively large quarries. Continue through *Chapel Stile,* which is at the centre of a vast parish. Holy Trinity Church celebrated its centenary in 1960, replacing a smaller structure.

The area was once managed by the monks of Furness, who are said to have had a place of worship in Little Langdale.

Great Langdale: The eye ranges across green fields by the river to where the Langdale Pikes stand like two battered sphinxes, rough and weather-seamed. Langdale appeals to climbers because of the great selection of rock faces that are near at hand. The climbs are nicely graded, from easy to very difficult. Scout Crag is mainly for beginners, and Tarn Crag is a grade stiffer. The really hard climbs, which continually fascinate the experts, are White Ghyll, Pavey Ark, Gimmer Crag and Bowfell Buttress. They form as fascinating a collection of seamed, sheer rock as you will find anywhere in Britain. Two hotels at the dalehead have *Dungeon Ghyll* in their titles. The roads tend to be narrow. Some car parking areas have been provided in recent years for casual visitors who do not visit the inns, but it is unwise to rely on finding a space at the peak of the year.

Blea Tarn and Little Langdale: The road from Great Langdale climbs in a zig-zag and passes close to Blea Tarn, with its attractive roadside farmhouse about which the poet Wordsworth wrote. The road descends to near the head of Little Langdale. Some motorists, turning right, follow the Wrynose Pass up to the point between here and the head of the Duddon valley where the Three Shires Stone stands as an ancient marker. Now, of course, the three counties that shared the Lake District — Cumberland, Westmorland and Lancashire — have been locally amalgamated as Cumbria. In any case, the Three Shires Stone is related only to Lancashire, the name being prominently marked upon it. The road down Little Langdale is narrow and winding; it should be followed with care.

Kirkstone and Troutbeck: Leave Ambleside by way of The Struggle, the road climbing steeply to:—

Kirkstone Pass Inn: Kirkstone Pass reaches a height of 1,476 feet, and the inn is not quite at the summit. It was granted its licence about 1840. The walls of the inn are some three feet thick; the roof is of durable local slate.

Here are the third highest licensed premises in England, giving way to the *Tan Hill Inn* and Derbyshire's *Cat and Fiddle.* The view from near the inn, looking westwards, is outstanding. Wordsworth wrote of Kirkstone Pass: "Who comes not hither ne'er shall know, how beautiful the world below". You see Windermere, with its wooded shores and islets; Blelham Tarn, which you might almost take for one of the great lake's many bays, and a distant panorama of gaunt fells. Morecambe Bay can be seen from a point near the inn.

Troutbeck: Travel southwards, with high-level views of the upper Troutbeck valley. Turn off the main road into Troutbeck village, which stretches as a succession of attractive buildings for a considerable distance along the hillside. At *Townend,* Troutbeck, is the old home of the Browne family, a house that is packed with carved oak. Owned by The National Trust, it is open to visitors at prescribed times. Townend is just as attractive outside as within, having dazzling white walls, mullion windows and distinctive circular chimneys.

The Brownes lived here from when the house was built in Tudor days until 1944, and they clearly loved their home. Here is the original Jacobean woodwork, all in oak; floors and wall panelling are also of oak. One of the bedroom floors is uneven, and the slope was naturally taken into account when a member of the family made an attractive four-poster bed, which has two legs longer than the others! In a bedroom is a framed family tree of the Brownes, made up of signatures taken from letters. The first is of George Browne, who was buried at Windermere in 1558.

Windermere and Bowness: St. Mary's church, Applethwaite, which is not far along the main road from the place where it is joined by the route from Troutbeck, was founded in 1848. Until the coming of the railway in 1847, there was just a small cluster of houses where Windermere now lies; the hamlet was called Birthwaite.

Bowness is by far the older place. *St. Martin's Church* dates back to 1483 and replaced an older building that was destroyed by fire. The stained glass includes pieces from

Cartmel Priory. One piece of glass may date from 1260, which makes it among the earliest existing coloured glass in England. Bowness Bay is thronged by pleasure craft and is also a calling point for the lake "steamers" of *Sealink.* The first steamer service began when the Windermere Steam Yacht Company was formed in 1845 and operated the "Lady of the Lake". At one time, there were two rival companies, and a "cold war" developed on the lake. Furness Railway bought the steamer service in 1871.

On the way back to Ambleside, stop for a while between Bowness and the main road to walk on *Queen Adelaide's Hill,* which has paths, seats — and outstanding views of Windermere.

The Wordsworth Country: Travel a few miles northwards from Ambleside, and you are in the area which William Wordsworth and his sister, Dorothy, commended to the world.

At *Rydal,* go first to the church, thence into The Rashfield, the one-and-a-half acre sloping field adjacent to the gardens of the Wordsworths' home, Rydal Mount. At one time the poet thought he would build a house here; he bought the land and gave it to his daughter, Dora, who also predeceased him. Today, visitors sometimes wonder at the name of the field; it relates to rushes. They can walk through it by courtesy of The National Trust, who received it from a grandson of the poet in 1935. The most attractive time is spring, and especially about the time of Wordsworth's birthday, April 7, when it is full of blossom from daffodil and narcissus.

Wordsworth helped to choose the site of *Rydal Church,* which was opened in 1824. *Rydal Mount,* home of the poet for 37 years, and the place where he died in 1850, is owned by the Rydal Mount Trust Limited, and on April 7, 1970 — the bi-centenary of Wordsworth's birth — Rydal Mount was opened to the public for the first time. On the way to Grasmere, a motorist passes close to the reed-edged *Rydal Water.*

Grasmere was the name originally given to the lake, of course. It probably meant "the lake with the grass shores", though some authorities have associated it with *gris,* for pig.

The lake that eventually gave its name to the parish is only a mile long and half a mile broad, but like many valley lakes it has considerable depth, nearly 80 feet. There is an island. Grasmere — also applied to the village — has absorbed an assembly of mini-communities: Town Head, Easedale, Back o' t'Lake, Churchtown and Town End.

Wordsworth lived at Town End and used this name as his address. The building was later known as *Dove Cottage,* and today it is at the centre of interest for those who want to learn about the remarkable family. William and Dorothy Wordsworth lived here for eight years; William brought his bride, Mary Hutchinson, to this place in 1802, three children were born here. The plain, whitewashed building with its constricted living space is generally associated with Wordsworth's finest years as a poet.

Dove Cottage is "open to view" at prescribed times, and associated with it is the nearby *Wordsworth Museum;* a combined admission ticket is issued. Here are objects, domestic and farming, from the period when Wordsworth lived and, upstairs, has been assembled what is probably the finest collection of Wordsworthiana. Students who wish to consult books and manuscripts can apply to the Trust for permission.

A vast number of visitors enter the *Churchyard* at Grasmere to see where Wordsworth and his kith and kin were buried. The graves are of William (died 1850), Mary his wife (1859), their daughter Dora (who married Edward Quillian), Dorothy and two children who died in 1812 when, for a brief period, the Wordsworths lived at the Rectory.

(For full details of Wordsworth's life and work in the area, consult "Grasmere and the Wordsworths", published by "Dalesman".)

Hawkshead: Anyone interested in Wordsworth who wishes to undertake a pilgrimage to the places associated with him should not overlook Hawkshead, the quaint village standing a few miles to the south-west of Ambleside, near the head of Esthwaite Water. William Wordsworth attended the grammar school and at Hawkshead he lodged with Anne Tyson. The schoolhouse, which can be visited, looks venerable, with its roughcast walls, heavy slate roof and cylindrical chimney. There is an attractive sundial over the door.

The original school was founded by the Sandys family in 1585, and it ceased to be used as a school in 1909. Most visitors look for the name of Wordsworth which was cut on a desk by the poet himself (history does not tell us whether or not he was chastised for this act of vandalism.)

For some idea of the social and farming conditions of Wordsworth's day, see the folk museum which has been established in the *Courthouse* at Hawkshead.

Norwegian-style building, between Ambleside and Waterhead

NATIONAL PARK CENTRE

A little to the south of Ambleside, presiding over a small estate which extends to the shores of Windermere, is Brockhole, the Lake District National Park Centre. It should be visited early in a holiday for basic information about the Lake District : the geology, history, vegetation, topography, land use and, of course, about the National Park, which consists of 866 square miles of hill, dale and lake.

In a house the Gaddums built are exhibitions telling the story of the Lake District from the earliest geological times to the daily life of the present day. There is a cafe, in which 100 people can be comfortably seated under a roof that is timber-lined, topped off with local slate. A great number of visitors arrive by water, in boats from Bowness that call at the jetty; they stride along a path between trees to open ground (part of the 32 acre estate) and see the old home of the Gaddums, white, elegant, above terraces where, in spring, azaleas and rhododendrons bloom. There is blossom somewhere at any time of the year. The Gaddums were wealthy Manchester manufacturers. They had both the money and the taste to build well. Mawson, landscape gardener of Windermere, was commissioned to lay out the gardens, which he did effectively. Visitors have access to no less than a third of a mile of lake shore.

Brockhole does not exist in a vacuum. In and around it is a miscellany of birds and animals typical of Lakeland. A watcher on the shore sees the sandpiper and red-breasted merganser each nesting season. Cormorants are among the birds that fly along Windermere within easy viewing distance. In the woods are jays and woodpeckers. The odd buzzard, kestrel or sparrow-hawk hunts hopefully around the estate. A nest-box scheme with the co-operation of the Cumbria Naturalists' Trust has encouraged the pied flycatcher to become well established. Red squirrels may be seen in the grounds.

The whole of the ground floor of Brockhole is devoted to the main exhibition, telling the Lakeland story in models, pictures and with full use of audio-visual aids. A large, imaginatively-devised model shows the Lake District as it might have been during the latter days of the Ice Ages, with glaciers in many of the valleys.

The farmer, so often overlooked by those writing about Lakeland, is seen as the man who sustains the basic industry, agriculture. One section of the main exhibition relates to the construction and maintenance of drystone walls. The main exhibitions are designed for adults, but children in parties from primary schools have their own room. Brockhole makes it available to teachers, who here can either use their own methods of delivery and their own information about the Lake District, or make use of prepared talks and slide shows.